Withdrawn

P9-DFQ-101

APR 0 9 2018

Northville District Library
212 W. Cady Street
Northville, MI 48167-1560

A Day at the
Beach
Animal Life
on the Shore

Bloodworms

and Other Wriggly Beach Dwellers

by Ellen Lawrence

Consultant:

Matt Bentley, FLS FRSB
Professor of Marine Biology
Newcastle University
Singapore

BEARPORT
PUBLISHING

New York, New York

Credits

Cover, © age fotostock/Shutterstock; 2, © Alexander Semenov/Science Photo Library; 4T, © Leon Werdinger/Alamy; 4B, © Ekaterina Pokrovsky/Shutterstock; 5, © Gianpiero Ferrari/FLPA; 6, © age fotostock/Alamy; 7, © Daniel L. Geiger/SNAP/Alamy; 7B, © Daniel L. Geiger/SNAP/Alamy; 8, © David Fenwick; 9, © age fotostock/Alamy; 10, © Mikkel Juul Jensen/Science Photo Library; 11L, © Astrid & Hanns-Frieder Michler/Science Photo Library; 11, © Blanscape/Shutterstock; 12, © Arterra Picture Library/Alamy; 13, © imageBROKER/Alamy; 14, © Nick Upton/Nature Picture Library; 15, © K Byrne/Alamy; 16, © Flonline/FLPA; 17L, © D P Wilson/FLPA; 17, © Erica Olsen/FLPA; 18, © Steve Gschmeissner/Science Photo Library; 19, © Alexander Semenov/Science Photo Library; 20, © Wim Van Egmond/Science Photo Library; 21, © Frank Greenaway/Getty Images; 22L, © Niall Benvie/Alamy; 22R, © Bundit Yuwannasiri/Shutterstock; 23TL, © Jacek Wojnarowski/Shutterstock; 23TC, © Colorshadow/Shutterstock; 23TR, © Sirithattu/Shutterstock; 23BL, © Vojce/Shutterstock; 23BC, © Flonline/FLPA; 23BR, © David Fenwick.

Publisher: Kenn Goin
Senior Editor: Joyce Tavolacci
Creative Director: Spencer Brinker
Photo Researcher: Ruth Owen Books

Library of Congress Cataloging-in-Publication Data

Names: Lawrence, Ellen, 1967– author.
Title: Bloodworms and other wriggly beach dwellers / by Ellen Lawrence.
Description: New York, New York : Bearport Publishing, [2018] | Series: A day
   at the beach: animal life on the shore | Includes
   bibliographical references and index.
Identifiers: LCCN 2017048987 (print) | LCCN 2017052928 (ebook) |
ISBN 9781684025022 (Ebook) | ISBN 9781684024445 (library)
Subjects: LCSH: Seashore animals—Juvenile literature. | Intertidal
   organisms—Juvenile literature. | Seashore ecology—Juvenile literature. |
   Beaches—Juvenile literature.
Classification: LCC QH95.7 (ebook) | LCC QH95.7 .L3586 2018 (print) | DDC
   578.769/9—dc23
LC record available at https://lccn.loc.gov/2017048987

Copyright © 2018 Bearport Publishing Company, Inc. All rights reserved. No part of this publication may be reproduced in whole or in part, stored in any retrieval system, or transmitted in any form or by any means, electronic, mechanical, photocopying, recording, or otherwise, without written permission from the publisher.

For more information, write to Bearport Publishing Company, Inc., 45 West 21st Street, Suite 3B, New York, New York 10010. Printed in the United States of America.

Contents

Secret Beach Dwellers

At the seashore, seagulls soar in the sky and crabs crawl over sand.

However, some seashore animals live secret lives.

These wriggly beach dwellers are **marine** worms that mostly stay hidden underground.

The only clues they leave behind are holes and **castings** in the muddy sand!

worm

wormholes and castings

oystercatcher

worm

Many different
kinds of worms might live
on a single beach. Seagulls,
oystercatchers, and other
seabirds feed on the
juicy worms.

Going Hunting!

A fierce hunter called a bloodworm lives on many beaches.

This worm can grow to be more than 12 inches (30.5 cm) long!

It moves through the sand hunting for beach fleas and small **shellfish**.

Once the bloodworm finds a meal, it attacks.

It shoots an alien-like mouthpart called a proboscis (proh-BOS-uhss) out of its head!

bloodworm

head

A bloodworm gets its name from its reddish-pink color. The worm's skin, however, is actually clear. The red color comes from the worm's blood showing through its skin.

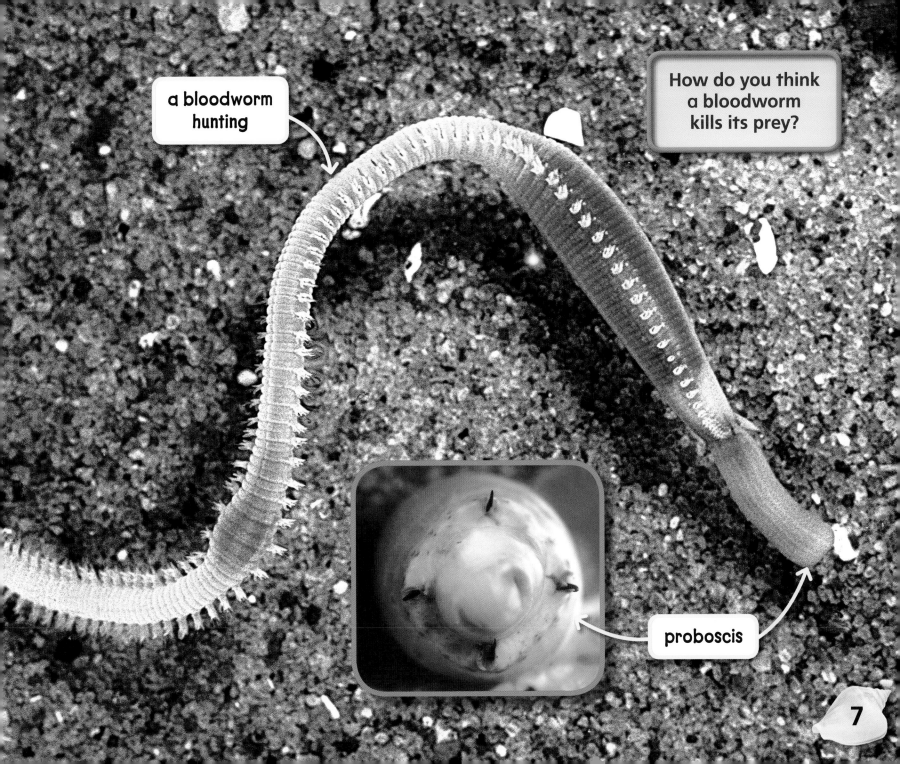

7

Fierce Fangs

As a bloodworm attacks, four fangs shoot from its proboscis.

The worm sinks its razor-sharp teeth into its prey's body.

Powerful **venom** flows from the fangs into the worm's victim.

The venom **paralyzes** the animal but doesn't kill it.

Then the hungry worm eats its prey while the animal is still alive!

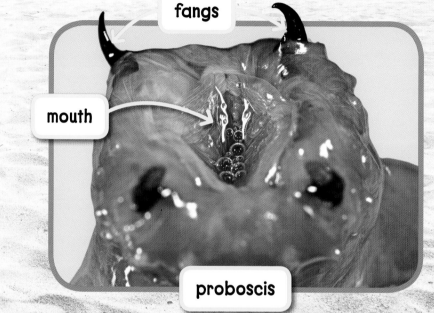

fangs

mouth

proboscis

A bloodworm actually has metal fangs! Each fang contains small amounts of copper—the same metal used to make pennies.

segments

An adult bloodworm's body is made up of hundreds of segments, or sections.

Meet a Lugworm

Another wriggly beach creature is a lugworm.

This sea animal looks like an earthworm with one skinny end.

It pushes its body into the sand, creating a U-shaped burrow.

As it lies in its burrow, a lugworm eats wet sand.

Mixed in with the sand are tiny bits of food.

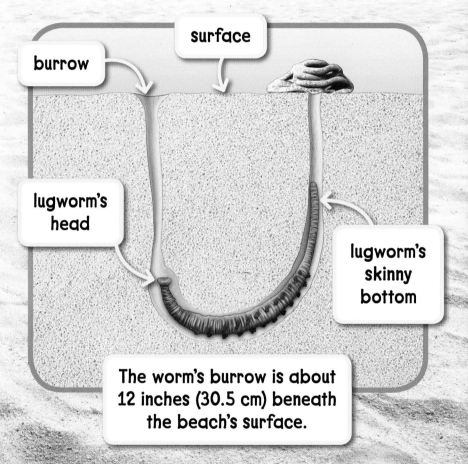

burrow

surface

lugworm's head

lugworm's skinny bottom

The worm's burrow is about 12 inches (30.5 cm) beneath the beach's surface.

The sand that a lugworm eats contains very tiny animals and plantlike living things called diatoms. The worm also eats bits of dead animals and seaweed.

lugworm castings

The diatoms in this picture are more than 50 times bigger than they are in real life.

Above a lugworm's burrow is a pile of castings. How do you think the worm makes these?

11

Sandy Spaghetti

As a lugworm eats sand, it creates a small hole on the beach.

Near the hole, a heap of castings that look like spaghetti pile up.

The castings are the lugworm's poop!

The worm eats sand, and then poops out long, sandy castings.

A lugworm sometimes poops every 40 minutes!

lugworm hole

lugworm poop

a lugworm that's been dug out of the sand

Like a fish, a lugworm breathes through body parts called gills.

Sand Mason Worms

What's that strange tube poking out of the sand?

It's the home of a sand mason worm!

The worm makes the tube from sand and tiny bits of seashells.

It sticks the pieces together with glue from its body.

At the end of the tube are tiny, branchlike parts.

the tube of a sand mason worm

A sand mason worm is about 12 inches (30.5 cm) long. Its tube can be up to 17 inches (45 cm) long, and most of it is buried under the sand.

branchlike parts

tiny pieces
of shell

tube

15

Tentacle Time!

Once the tide comes in and water covers the beach, a sand mason worm is ready to eat.

Sticky **tentacles** appear from the end of its tube.

The worm uses its tentacles to catch tiny animals and plants floating in the water.

Once the tide goes out, the worm slides back down into its tube.

This keeps it safe from seabirds that want to eat it.

tentacles

a sand mason worm outside of its tube

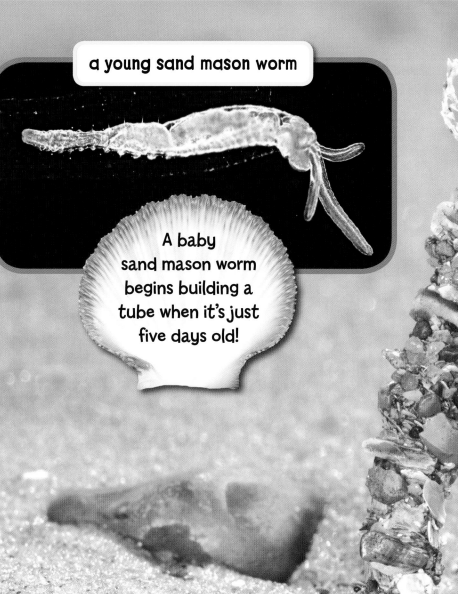

a young sand mason worm

A baby sand mason worm begins building a tube when it's just five days old!

the tube of a sand mason worm

How do you think a sand mason worm repairs its tube if it breaks?
(The answer is on page 24.)

King of Worms

One of the biggest worms at the beach is the 3-foot (91 cm) long king ragworm.

This worm spends its time in its burrow or searching for food.

It will eat almost anything—including dead animals.

When a ragworm finds prey, it grabs the animal with its fangs.

Then the worm gobbles down its meal!

fangs

a close-up photo of a ragworm's jaws

A ragworm has hundreds of tiny, leglike parts called parapods. They help the worm crawl through the sand. They also contain the worm's gills. So the animal breathes through its legs!

king ragworm

head

parapods

19

Baby Ragworms

Male and female ragworms meet up in the sea to have young.

The female ragworm releases eggs into the water.

Tiny ragworm larvae hatch from the eggs.

The larvae swim in the sea, growing bigger every day.

Finally, they begin their adult lives in their sandy home!

ragworm larva

a king ragworm burrowing into the sand

A female king ragworm can lay millions of eggs at one time. After having young, adult ragworms die.

Science Lab

Be a Marine Worm Scientist!

Scientists have studied beach worms for many years. Now it's your turn to investigate! Read the following questions and write your answers in a notebook.

I. The lugworm shown here is life-size. How long is the worm?

(To measure the worm, first lay a piece of string along its body. Then use a ruler to measure the string.)

2. What do you think is happening in the picture below?

3. Write one paragraph about the life of a sand mason worm. Try to use the following words:

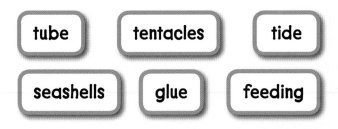

tube   tentacles   tide

seashells   glue   feeding

(The answers are on page 24.)

Science Words

castings (KAST-ingz)
waste that is passed out of
a worm's body after it eats

marine (muh-REEN)
having to do with the
sea

paralyzes (PA-ruh-lize-iz)
causes an animal to be
unable to move

shellfish (SHEL-fish)
ocean animals with
a shell, such as crabs,
shrimp, and mussels

tentacles (TEN-tuh-kuhlz)
long, armlike body parts
used by some animals for
grasping food, feeling, or
moving

venom (VEN-uhm)
poison that is injected
into an animal through
a bite or sting

Index

Read More

Moore, Heidi. *Giant Tube Worms and Other Interesting Invertebrates (Creatures of the Deep).* Chicago: Raintree (2012).

Owen, Ruth. *Welcome to the Seashore (Nature's Neighborhoods: All About Ecosystems).* New York: Ruby Tuesday (2016).

Spilsbury, Richard and Louise. *A Nature Walk on the Beach (Read and Learn).* Chicago: Heinemann (2015).

Learn More Online

To learn more about worms at the beach, visit **www.bearportpublishing.com/ADayAtTheBeach**

About the Author

Ellen Lawrence lives in the United Kingdom. Her favorite books to write are those about nature and animals. In fact, the first book Ellen bought for herself when she was six years old was the story of a gorilla named Patty Cake that was born in New York's Central Park Zoo.

Answers

Page 17: The worm can turn around in its tube. It uses its tentacles to grab sand and bits of seashells from the water. Finally, the worm makes repairs with these materials.

Page 22:
1. The worm is 9.4 inches (24 cm) long.

2. The picture shows castings, or poop, coming out of a lugworm. Look closely, and you can see the worm's yellow bottom sticking out of the wet sand.